The Swimmer

The Swimmer

Poems by Susan Ludvigson

Louisiana State University Press
Baton Rouge and London
1984

Designer: Joanna Hill
Typeface: ITC Garamond
Typesetter: G & S Typesetters, Inc.
Printer: Thomson-Shore
Binder: John Dekker & Sons

The author gratefully acknowledges the editors of the following magazines, in
which many of the poems herein first appeared: *Atlantic Monthly*, *Black
Warrior Review*, *Crazy Horse*, *Devil's Millhopper*, *Foot(hill) Notes*, *Georgia
Review*, *Illuminations*, *Kansas Quarterly*, *Outlet*, *Poetry*, *Poetry Miscellany*,
Southern Poetry Review, *Virginia Quarterly Review*.

The author would also like to thank the Virginia Center for the Creative Arts,
where many of these poems were written, and to express her gratitude to
Kathryn Kirkpatrick, Julie Suk, and Stephen Corey for their generous and
valuable criticisms of the manuscript. And the author wants to thank Rebekah
Wade for the newspaper clippings stolen from her refrigerator door, which
provided ideas for several of these poems.

Library of Congress Cataloging in Publication Data

Ludvigson, Susan.
  The swimmer.
    I. Title.
PS3562.U27S9 1984   811'.54   83-25593
ISBN 0-8071-1155-4
ISBN 0-8071-1172-4 (pbk.)

Dedicated to the memory of

Lawrence D. Joiner   1939–1981

Anne Royall Newman   1925–1982

Arnold M. Shankman   1946–1983

Contents

III Crossing

I
Grief

Every single angel is terrible!

Rilke, *First Duino Elegy*

Grief

Imagine that pure
melting of snow in Wisconsin
so that when it's gone, the earth
underneath is raw and damp,
needing sun, seed, any kind
of promise. But more snow comes
before the final thaw,
and this goes on, over and over,
so that in February, March,
you think the world may never
be green.
When you look out the picture window,
after your spirits have risen one last
slow time, old grass looks
as if it might leap to life.
Then you see those large flakes
floating down, and you weep,
past belief. It can happen
through April, hope going white
and silent again.

Water on water in perfect fusion,
light welded to shimmering light.
When the thunder started, and the lightning,
I tried to remember the horses my father lost
to a storm, struck in the nearest pasture.
Absorbed in the pleasure of water,
I had to work hard at fear, that dark savior,
to make myself head for shore.

Some Notes on Courage

Think of a child who goes out
into the new neighborhood,
cap at an angle, and offers to lend
a baseball glove. He knows
how many traps there are—
his accent or his clothes, the club
already formed.
Think of a pregnant woman
whose first child died—
her history of blood.
Or your friend whose father
locked her in basements, closets,
cars. Now when she speaks
to strangers, she must have
all the windows open.
She forces herself indoors each day,
sheer will makes her climb the stairs.
And love. Imagine it. After all
those years in the circus, that last
bad fall when the net didn't hold.
Think of the ladder to the wire,
spotlights moving as you move,
then how you used to see yourself
balanced on the shiny air.
Think of doing it again.

Doves cooing in unison ask them,
and with my bad eyes, their bodies
are curved marks in the air.

I find myself shrugging, lifting my hands
to the brittle sky, half-expecting
a piece to break off and crash
into the pool, to float transparent,
blue on blue.

Months ago this patch of land was gold,
ready for harvest. Now, in the midst
of green, the usual crops don't grow.
Rain might result from the simple absence
of sun, or something sinister—
acid in the air, messages there's no code for.

Love is mysterious as mushrooms.
I follow those who know
the dangerous kinds, who can pluck
what's safe from the mass of sprouts,
those wild enticing morsels.
Even up close, and after instruction,
I can't be sure.
In my ignorant hands
even the obviously poison
masquerades as pure.

Leaving

Through all those nights,
a man's breath measuring
the minutes, his presence
the completion of the room,
she believed that alone she would
fly apart, a milkweed pod,
to drift on the blackness
like half-formed stars.
Sometimes, stepping carefully
across the red carpet, trying
not to wake him, she'd feel
the color in the soles
of her feet, wish herself suffused
with red. Then she could slip
into an evening, find the depot,
disappear to Canada or California.
But she needed dawn to consider it.
Finally, she had to imagine
Norway, to dream of the long light
holding her, like a mother,
in its arms, to feel it fill
her body and stay there, where
just by thinking, she could
make dew form on the grass,
and the trees shine.

The Night We Sang

The night we sang until 3 A.M.
my back hurt so much
I thought splinters were lodged
near my spine, reminders
that floors, like certain beds,
can be dangerous. Yours, for instance,
though in fact that time the cause
was undramatic: I'd merely
leaned to pick up a pillow.
After dinner, drunk by the fire,
we remembered the piano—
first Bach, and then show tunes,
then old southern hymns.
We distressed the air
in those proper rooms
like ghosts encountering
uncovered mirrors,
their souls lost forever.

I reminded you of our first night
together, how you'd shamed me with all
my Sunday School talk,
making me sing a childish verse
that proved, you said,
what a prude I was.

When we found that old book
with its tattered cover, its black notes
like birds on the autumn sky,
the music absorbed our reckless voices
(we were hoarse for two days), absorbed
my pain, your desire, the dark
we hadn't seen coming in.

The Man Who Can't Love

He lives in the valley of regret,
where the trees cast shadows
all day long.
Even when he takes the rowboat
out to the smooth lake
where the fish are biting
and the afternoon sun makes the whole
world glow, he can't forget
how pleasure, that leisurely drift
to a sandbar with beer and a woman,
leads him back to the furtive
hiding in closets, watching his mother
undress. Always he waits
for something to change,
for the everyday world of babies,
of trips to the beach, of fathers
who dream of retirement,
to bless him, to make *marriage*
a word for *love*, to make love transcend
his guilty palms on breasts
and become "what the angels do."

I Arrive in a Small Boat, Alone

In my bed your body is an island
inhabited by a cautious race of men
whose elaborate rituals were designed
for safety, like the shaking of hands
to show an absence of weapons,
or the sharing of food to prove its purity.
They are united, they rally
to a common cause, so that
when possible danger appears,
they line up, each with one knee
on the ground for balance,
shields side by side,
the reflected sun bright enough
to blind the approaching figure,
me, waving a hand.
Now and then one's caught by himself
off-duty, the tribe's chant
dim in the distance. Sometimes
he hears a song that seems
to come from his own blood's rhythm.
But he checks himself,
returns to the village quickly,
rarely tripping on roots,
for he's memorized the path,
cut away offending branches.
Safely back, he joins the others,

sleeps in his own hut, in tune
with the breath of his brothers.
He knows if he keeps still long enough
the music will stop.

The Sabotage of Dreams

Night encourages darkness to rise
from the bottom where, in the heaviest
water, everything's silent,
patient as submarines.

On the road home, asleep at the wheel,
you know you must wake,
and do, to buildings careening,
death near as the hill where your house was
before the highway shifted and spread
like tree roots growing beyond their boundaries,
cracking the solid foundation.

The same week, a policeman behind a window
triggers his own persistent nightmare
and your young son's face explodes.

Your daytime life is as quiet
as that Spanish sea where you drifted
far from the coast,
the fish so near you could watch
as they'd glisten toward bread
you tossed on the shimmering surface.

He says he's all darkness, wishes he could care.
I am not wanton, don't fling myself at men,
but fell into his arms as if despair

were the proper price. Now what I hastily spent
I want to earn back. Yet only small coins
rattle in my heart. I take up pen

and try to write it, to understand the point,
like peering through binoculars to the church
five miles away. The picture's out of joint

here in the mountain retreat where birch
and maple absorb the night sounds
of animals, of human grief. Later today I'll search

for the moth, note the beauty of the luna's down
against its ugly body, that iridescent green
pulsing its last on the log's crown

where I watched it yesterday. I'll look to trees
for answers, as if nature stored them up
to be discovered by any stray hiker, free.

This at a time when death's buzzing shop
is open all hours. Three friends give up the fight,
almost, with cancer. I have to work hard to stop

imagining them in a craftsman's hands, light
wood he carves into shapes, torsos of pain
whittled clean. Everywhere I look, tight-

lipped patients, doctors, families strain
for belief. But the miracles we half-expect of love
go whistling off on the nearest train,

denying failure. I put on the sterile gloves
and mask, tell myself this has nothing
to do with me. Then, shaken with fear, shove

the bouquets aside and admit it: Breathing
is precious as any dream of the future.
Everything pales in the whispering,

the request for a simple back rub, a gesture
that's useful. I observe the odd fragrance, alcohol and
     sweat.
Something here is genuine. Not that mixture

of lust and need we grasp for and sometimes guess
is all. If there is anything like a way out,
it's discovered in rooms like these, pressed

as we are to be honest, at least to ourselves, about
love, though sickness keeps growing like doubt.

Tracking the Deer

After the age of forty, when a man shoots a deer, and he walks
over to the deer, he's *in* the deer.
Robert Bly

That single glimpse of him
through the birch
misleads: he's agile as a fawn,
but wiser,
and when the hard snows come
he knows how long he'll last.
We trudge through the woods
watching our silent breath
until the brightness
starts us bantering again.
We nearly forget where we are,
how this moment is a museum landscape,
animals striking the same
stiff perfect poses.

Anne, Dying

Her body like a stubborn root
dug up and left in the air to dry
has survived and survived,
but now that will, like her caught breath,
is nearly gone.

Pain spills through her like blood
from the heart the cancer grows against,
surrounds, tough lilies of the valley
spreading until their sweetness
overpowers, crowding the bed
so nothing else can feel the sun.

Love comes trooping in with baskets
of white flowers, an awful innocence.
It fails. It masquerades as hope,
believes itself awhile, and in the end,
does not save anyone.

Prayer

Fear brightens her eyes more than the drugs.
I expected dullness,
but remember my father, alive with morphine
and plans for a way to move his legs again.
Now she lies beneath damp sheets,
the third set today,
and waits.

Feathers of light rise on the moving air,
higher and higher, the blue becoming thinner
until it's dazzling white,
a rich emptiness like the moments
after love. I wish it for my dying friend,
my dead father. I keep trying to say
how we disappear, and hope it's so.

I would see them lifted into a promise,
something beyond our earthly dream for them,
the simple absence of pain.

A Day of Snow

It's not the world I care about now,
but a few lives.
Yours. Mine. The friends
who go on dying.
After Don, after Anne,
I can hardly believe how it continues.
But Tom's Christmas card says so,
and Roy's disease has switched names
and places, become leukemia,
and Arnold gets thinner
as the chemicals glide
through his veins, damaging
his heart like broken promises.
And you are somewhere else
with a woman who loves you,
and whom you love, though not
the way we've known—explosions
of light through the body.
I'm here alone, thinking of the blizzard
that killed my cousin only weeks ago,
thinking how quiet snow is,
how grief is always white.

II
Escape

Then how I'd like to hide from this great longing!

Rilke, *Sixth Duino Elegy*

My Advice

To go out of your one body,
the one your husband toasts with champagne
on his birthday, making you smile,
the one children cling to,
annoyed at any change in its contours,
you must think of your hair another color,
blonde or gray, perhaps,
if it's auburn. Then imagine
yourself a farm wife, getting up
to milk, the sun coming pale as grapefruit
behind hills heavy with snow.
You can hear the cows moaning
from the barn, your man's
slow steps in the kitchen, the rattle
of a coffee pot. There might be peace
in this, or resentment. You decide.

Or, for an hour, you could become a man,
one you saw in a photograph
last week. Stranger or grandfather,
his secrets attract you.
Close your eyes. That weekend
you spend in the city
you gamble a fortune away
and nearly lose your youngest daughter,
as in the fairy tale. But luck
returns, and the woman in silk
who drives her own horses

and rubs your back with her strong
white fingers almost lures you
to Atlanta. You can see the pearls
on her bodice, hear that rustle
of blue as she leaves your room
the last time.

To change your one life
you need only enter another:
a ten-year-old child in Chicago.
Your parents dead of a fire,
you claim a happy life.
You'll see the all-night diner
where you've learned the cook's habits,
which customer leaves half his steak.
Bacon spits from the grill
as someone talks of a river in Minnesota,
thousands of speckled trout.

I, Leopold Trouvelot, am guilty,
though I meant no crime, and could not imagine
the apple, basswood, poplar and willow
gone, had not foreseen the loss of hawthorn
and sassafras. Only the butternut
still stands in my old field, a sentinel,
and a single dogwood sighs near the house
we had to leave. My Boston neighbors believed
I was sent by the devil, but it isn't so.
No god, either. I alone am responsible.

I saw silk in my dreams, flowing blue silk
wrapped twice round Marie, trailing her down
the stairs like water. *To make silk*, I thought,
more perfect than petals.
I remember Marie in the yard after dinner,
her long hair wound at the base of her neck
like a rose. She loved the grape arbor
and that white clapboard house
so different from our cottage back home.
She was happy, and I, with my secret project,
rejoiced.

But in May, the white flowers on the shadbush
opened, the oak leaves unfurled,
and my small friends betrayed me.
As the air got warmer,
the town began to fill with black worms

blown tree to tree on the strands they'd spun,
and in weeks most all the leaves disappeared.
Not even Paris green deterred them.
One woman we knew scraped worms
from the sides of her house
and into a pan, poured kerosene over and set them
on fire. All day long she did this, weeping.

Even here in France I can't forget.
Those caterpillars with red and blue warts
became the most hated sight in New England—
next to me. In my nightmares, oak leaves turn
in an instant to excrement. Yet sometimes I still dream
of innocent moths that float through my nights
like cherry blossoms, of incredible silk
lovely as Marie.

Darwin Discovers the Galapagos

Finding this place was like falling
into the moon. As a child I'd lie
on the hill beside our house at dusk
watching it brighten, those craters
caves I ached to explore. I imagined
every shadow a mystery
longing for light.

Now here I am, off the coast of Ecuador,
where an archipelago of volcanos,
land pocked as that ancient face,
greets me like a dream
of all I ever knew.

It *must* have begun here,
where everything's moon and sea.
Look—that bird can't lift into air
but dives through water
for its prey, flies beneath the waves
as if the breakers were clouds.
Even the odd iguanas, those tiny dinosaurs,
swim.

How many million years?

Here, where the equator cuts through
like a current, these steamy islands
have kept the story whole. I almost believe

it *is* dream. In the mangrove forests,
on the beaches where each grain of sand
is white as a star, in the lagoons
with their pink flamingos rising
out of the mist, I sometimes
have to grab Fitz by the shoulder
and demand to know what he sees.

Confirmed, I go off alone
to sit on the rocks and watch the sea lions slide
from the shore, the giant tortoises drift by,
to think of the words I might use
to tell the world of the world.

Conquering the Night Jasmine

Beneath the dining room window
where everyone knows it should never
be grown, the night jasmine sends up
its devilish fragrance, sweet
as anything God imagined—
but with that telltale underscent
of abandon, of clove.

I must eat before eight each evening,
before it begins to exhale through the screen,
making the dinner inedible,
peas, lamb and rice all honeyed alike.

Plain as a weedy potato vine,
it looks innocent all day,
its silence a dare
to accuse or uproot it.

I wouldn't. I know temptation
when I see it, and how to pass such tests.

Cestrum nocturnum, Cestrum nocturnum
I chant, and by nine it invades
the whole house, so all the air's sugary,
vulgar.

When I can bring
great panicles of the flowers in

as if they were fall hydrangeas, the tiny blooms
loose in Aunt Ellen's cranberry vase,
it will be victory.

I long for the hot summer night
I can keep my heart quiet
without the aid of marigolds.

Man Arrested in Hacking Death Tells Police
He Mistook Mother-in-Law for Raccoon

Every morning she'd smear something brown
over her eyes, already bagged
and dark underneath, as if that would
get her sympathy. She never slept,
she said, but wandered like a phantom
through the yard. I knew it. Knew
how she knelt beneath our bedroom window too,
and listened to Janet and me.

One night when *again* Janet said No,
I called her a cow, said she might as well
be dead for all she was good to me.
The old lady had fur in her head
and in her ears,
at breakfast slipped and told us
she didn't think the cows would die.

Today when I caught her
in the garage at dawn, that dyed hair
growing out in stripes, eyes
like any animal surprised from sleep
or prowling where it shouldn't be,
I did think, for a minute,
she was the raider of the garden,
and the ax felt good, coming down
on a life like that.

After Warnings from County Prosecutor Minister Agrees to Stop Using Electric Shocks to Teach Bible Students

Tried half my life
to fuse flesh and spirit,
finally learned how.

Listen, it's the joy
of a dry dive
into spring-fed, icy water,
but better, the reverse—
hot as a fever dream.

One girl *begs* me for the juice,
says when He enters her like that,
it's the moon exploding.
I can see every nerve amazed
with exquisite pain,
and in a flash
she knows the universe
inside out.

I swear, it's *wrong, wrong*
to condemn pure Christian ecstasy
as if it were sin.

His Confession

> The Health Department said 687 men and 520 females suffered
> bites from human beings last year.

Naturally, I thought she'd keep quiet.

I was careful about the places—
back of a thigh when she was sleeping so hard
she'd forgotten our fight
and cried out from her dream, later reporting
packs of wolves, and knives her father flashed.
Days after, she discovered
the bruises were real, but by then
the teeth marks were gone
and I was almost innocent.
Silly, I'd say, examining the raised
discolored flesh. *It could have been
anything.* I showed her my own
mysterious scars, and she whimpered
into her coffee.

But tonight, after I'd seen her drinking
again at the tavern with Ned, and when
she came home and suggested swimming,
my teeth ached. I dived under
as she floated on her back, that long body
like a trail of lilies, and when my jaws
found her drifting calf, it was supposed
to be a cramp, the kind I'd warned her about
for years. I expected we'd fold and knot
together, churning the water the way
a gator flails with an Irish setter.
But she was too damned sober.

After He Called Her a Witch

Special powers were attributed to the orange in Renaissance England, Italy, and Sicily. It was believed witches could bring death to an enemy by pinning the victim's name to an orange and leaving the orange in a chimney.

When he comes in, late again,
the whole house smells wonderful,
but he can't quite recognize the scent.
The fire is almost out, a few ashes
flicker in the absent light,
and suddenly he recalls
his mother holding orange peels
over a flame, the singed skin
curling back like petals,
releasing that fragrance.
She did it daily, all one winter,
just for the pleasure.

He doesn't see on the hearth
the remains of paper, traces
of his name printed in clear
black ink. He wonders how his wife
knew about sweetening their rooms
with oranges, wonders whether it means
the air is cleared,
she wants to make up.
He breathes the evening in,
imagining her in bed, waiting for him,
forgiveness on her lips
like the taste of oranges.

The Artist

for Sheba Sharrow

She keeps her windows open,
refusing to fix the torn screen all summer.
Ignoring mosquitoes, she tolerates
brown-speckled spiders she finds
in her sheets, hoping for one small creature
banded in colors nobody's used.
She has learned to see in the faintest light
how the veins of a moth in Virginia
cross at angles different from all
she's observed, and in her absorption,
does not hear the man who slips out
of the woods, whose hands are like nets.
When he surprises her, cupping her breasts
from behind, she imagines, first,
that they're doves, and she sees them
on canvas, white feathers pulsing
against dark fingers.

Cleopatra

after the painting by Guido Reni

Asp bites nipple, no fooling around.
She's larger than love,
and when she turns that white face up,
one hand resting
in the basket of snakes and flowers,
the other guiding reptile to target
by its curly tail,
it's hard to think of Antony
caressing that ample skin.
She could be a saint.
Those pudgy fingers should fold
in prayer, not casually pluck a nut
as she holds the asp
like an awkward teacup.
Her passive mouth might never
have been kissed; those eyes, raised
heavenward, are the eyes
of a Georgia farmwife
claiming ecstasy, not knowing
quite what she's missed.

Nobleman with His Hand on His Chest
after the painting by El Greco

Sir, I too agree with Ignatius.
One should touch his heart at each sin,
and the remembrance of it.

But you are not penitent. Your eyes
have learned sadness,
how, by focusing on a spot in the glass,
you can say to yourself,
Here is a gentleman wan with grieving.
I am that man. Believe the fingers
resting on pain.

We know better, you and I.

You love how the white ruff circles,
how lace softens, flatters
that sternness, sets off
the appropriate black
beneath your somber face.

Your sins glitter like your sword,
ornate and handsome.
You take them out in the dark
to admire; in public, you
press them back into place.

The Garden of Earthly Delights

after the painting by Hieronymus Bosch

So understandable that you
would seek birds,
with their fiery feet,
the yellow-striped plumes,   .
and beaks that curve and point
like graceful fingers.
Their plump throats pulse
the way your bodies should.
But your faces say something's wrong.
You rest on those feathery backs,
pondering. Even without each other
you should find pleasure
just sitting on such spiny softness.
Why the glum looks
when you've got what you wanted—
bodies naked as eggs—alabaster,
obsidian skin, yours for the touching,
the taking. You open
your ravenous mouths for sweet fruit,
and it's there. But your hearts
are cool as the water
where everyone rises to gorgeous sin.

Keeping the Truth Alive

after drawings by Heinrich Kley

Before we settle in
let's find tiny elephants
to suckle me awhile,
and admit the lady was right
who saw the earth perched
on a turtle's back. To Wm. James,
who objected, politely asking
what the turtle stood on,
she sagely replied, "Ah,
it's no use, Mr. James.
It's turtles, all the way down."
The crafty penguin
serenading a woman on the ice,
an accordion of human bodies
moaning out of tune
as legs are split
and pumped together again,
even the rape by snail—
we've known them, known
what it's like to sit
on the sword's edge pleading,
or to hold a small squealing animal
by one leg in the air.
As the sated preacher sleeps
beneath the crucifix,
he dreams of real Christian poverty

and wakes aghast. We dream
what we can. With luck we might be
the naked couple straddling
the Orient Express
still bound for Paris.

III
Crossing

Look, I'm living.
            On what?
                        Neither my childhood
nor my future
            is growing smaller . . .
                        Being
in excess
            wells up
                        in my heart.

Rilke, *Ninth Duino Elegy*

The Crossing

To find, across the bridge of night,
one constant voice urging you over,
telling you where the loose stones are,
where the missing beam, you must
be willing to risk that journey
with your eyes blindfolded, your hands
in gloves. You must believe that close
on the other side is a room
prepared only for you. There a small
blue lamp will be shining, and books
piled on the table, ones you've
longed for, but nearly forgot.
All the while you're crossing, feet
hesitant and chilled, you must imagine
a high four-postered bed, layers
of quilts, that voice become a murmur,
the river at your back.

Artists' Colony, After My Friend's Death

Someone dreamed
of a Norwegian couple
giving a banquet, the waiter's tip
spread on the tray
so the guests would know
it was time to leave.

We are more subtle here.
When Sarah is lonely, she brings
balloons to the table, gives us
each a different color.
After breakfast, we release them
like wishes into the August sky.

Karen sorts her mail
sighing, tells us her husband
misses her voice. She never flirts
with anyone, but reads those letters
as if she were missing a secret,
something in code.

Arthur entertains us with hoaxes,
signs a famous writer's name
to a libelous essay, sends it
to the *Times*.
We love him as he intends,
our hands behind our backs
like the statue of Cupid in the yard,

rose thorns binding
those libidinous arms.

I also dream of Norway
where in the long season
when the light prevents dreaming,
a grandmother tends the fire
while I, a child, keep watch
out the window, believing
this could save our lives.

Swimming

The water is gracious as taffeta
folding out from you, streaming over.
In sunlight it dazzles the skin,
brilliantly blinds you for moments
that last as long as breath.
You know the dream of flying
is nothing to this.
You drift beneath the surface
like reflected clouds
in a quick wind.
This is the life that skims
the dark, trades
the desire to stay down
for the cool splash of voices
at the pool's edge.

Where We Are Never Lost

We learn to dive from Pete's raft,
naked in the late and shadowy light,
hoping to be seen, not as we are,
thirteen and gawky as cranes
across the lake,
but nymphs the neighbor boys
will recognize and love.

Sunfish flash in the boat like medals,
splash in the pail until the light
is penny colored and our names echo
over water like skipped stones,
the only other sound a squeaky oar.

Days are long as dreams.
From the island, the cabin is a lighthouse,
the water fathomless as the future
we swim into.

Encounter at the Harbor

Everyone who made you what you are
appears in windows along the waterfront,
each with his own story, her own wish
for forgiveness. Your father
tells the assembly how you played
a music box over and over
until he thought he'd go mad
with the sweet tinny sound.
The nun who insisted you write
blasphemy a hundred times on the blackboard
drops her spectacles to the sidewalk,
urging the crowd to applaud as they shatter.
Your brother confirms his fascination
with your skin, how he teased you to silence,
making you let him touch you all over.
Someone recites a list of confessions,
why he invented a trip to Boston,
then disappeared like a pond in summer.
You stand before them dressed in white,
your face impassive as dawn.
Only when they weep in chorus
do you turn to the bay, point out
how the sun rises behind the island.

Deciding to Return

We are nearly at the shore now,
almost close enough to touch the reeds,
to spot the turtles lying like shadows
on roots lifted out of water.
In moments low-hanging leaves
will brush our faces in the dusk.
Too late to spot loons, to change
our minds and go back. Supper
is waiting. The cool raft is empty,
frogs are emerging, crickets
begin to sing.

Waiting for Light

These early mornings dark as water,
sleep drifts on the air, out of reach.
A man walks the spine of memory,
and I turn, in small pain,
on the too-soft mattress.
He might be snapping on a light
somewhere, shivering.
Might. Might have been.

The trees are beginning to shine.
I think of furniture, how
I rearranged a room last night,
making space for the old piano.
Impatient for light, I imagine
clumsy music, my fingers glad,
relearning the keys.

Virginia with Artists

for my friends at the VCCA

Now, in the summer of the secret dam
with its tiny lizard, that lovely iridescent tail,
my discovery of the word *catalpa*
and those bright broad leaves,
I think again of Spain, fields of poppies
spread across the green as if they were paintings

of themselves, splashes against the hills—paintings
direct from dreams. Here's the waterfall and dam
where in the dusk I half-expect poppies
or bougainvillea or orchids or cattails—
any bright soft foliage. There are real leaves
like fans, lacy mimosas and shiny catalpas

growing along these banks. Catalpa
trees surround the house, appear in paintings
of this place. I'm not ready to leave,
to put the summer behind me—nights at the dam
drifting in rowboats, bringing up the tail
end of each procession in the water. Poppies

don't belong here. Still I think of poppies
and Spain. I'd like to live with poppies and catalpas
long into fall, to stay in this tale
I tell myself, in the world of painting
and Chopin, retreats to the secluded dam,
the abstract renderings of leaves

that make photographs of those same leaves
mundane. Spain and remembered poppies
reshape themselves in my mind. I damn
the return to a city without mystery, without catalpas,
a landscape where paintings
and books provide the only fantasy, where I tail

behind in conversations that usually entail
politics, the news of the day. When everyone leaves,
I'll enter the room of my own paintings,
go straight to the Ammerman—huge, wonderful poppies.
I'll entertain myself, roll words like *catalpa*
quietly on my tongue, thinking back to the dam,

how we gathered leaves, touched the lizard's tail
just once and it fell off like poppies' petals, how paintings
alter everything. I see a dam, a shore dark with catalpas.

The Swimmer

Imagine yourself a strong swimmer.
Instead of that awkward crawl to the raft
you can go all the way out, then down to the dam
half a mile away. There's nothing in sight
to disturb you. No shiny rowboats, no walkers
along the shore like sentinels.
No sign of rain or shudder of thunder.
Only the gentlest ripples alter the surface,
the ghost of a breeze. You can keep on swimming
until the sun goes out like a candle.
Under that starry sky, you'll float
in the shadows of shadows.
There might be no end to it, just water
darkening into night, then slowly restoring itself
to blue. The silence will be a new entrance
to dreams, sleep a new way to breathe.